Our Story

In 2019, our founder, Stacy Padula, had been a published author for ten years. When her sixth book, *Gripped Part 1: The Truth We Never Told* was released, she received word from a producer that there was interest in adapting her books for screen. Although she had already finished writing the next two books in her series, her publisher was insistent on releasing the books six months apart. With an offer from Hollywood looming, Stacy felt it was imperative that the books be released sooner. This led her to put her industry experience to use and start Briley & Baxter Publications, LLC.

Named after Stacy's two loveable miniature dachshunds (who are by her side daily in the office), our company was founded with a mission to support animal rescues with a portion of its monthly royalties. Baxter, a rescue from Arkansas, was the inspiration behind this mission. Recipients have included organizations such as Last Hope K9 Rescue, the Wolf Conservation Center, WIRES Australian Wildlife Rescue, Dachshund Rescue of South Florida, Little Paws Dachshund Rescue, Tiny Tim On Wheels Foundation, Silicon Valley Pet Project, and Freedom Service Dogs of America.

In 2021, Stacy realized that opening up Briley & Baxter Publications to other writers would be an excellent way to raise funds for animal rescues and help aspiring authors achieve their dreams. She hired a team of experienced editors, illustrators, designers, and communications professionals to help her build our company into what it is today. To date, we have published over fifty titles in a variety of genres. Our books include many award-winning titles, and our authors range from high school students to retired professional athletes. Two of our series are currently being adapted for television, and we have many other titles in the works for 2023. We continue to seek out talented authors and artists whose work inspires readers to make our world a better place, one book at a time.

Contents

Readers' Choice Book Awards

Gold Winner: Best Teen Book, 2022
Gripped Part 1: The Truth We Never Told by Stacy A. Padula

Silver Winner: Best Teen Book, 2022
Gripped Part 5: Taylor's Story by Stacy A. Padula

Silver Winner: Best Children's Book (Ages 3-7), 2023
Stars of the North by Lucy Kovaliv

Silver Winner: Best Children's Book (Ages 8-12), 2023
I Love Dandelions by August E. Allen

Finalist: Best Teen Book, 2023
Montgomery Lake High #1: The Right Person by Stacy A. Padula

Finalists: Best Children's Book, 2022 & 2023
The Adventures of Owen & the Anthem Singer by Rachel Goguen & Todd Angilly
The Colors Inside of Me by AmyLee Westervelt
The Lighthouse Keeper Saves the Bay by Teddy Biron
On the Right Path: Book Two by Brett Gunning & Stacy A. Padula
On the Right Path: Book Three by Brett Gunning & Stacy A. Padula

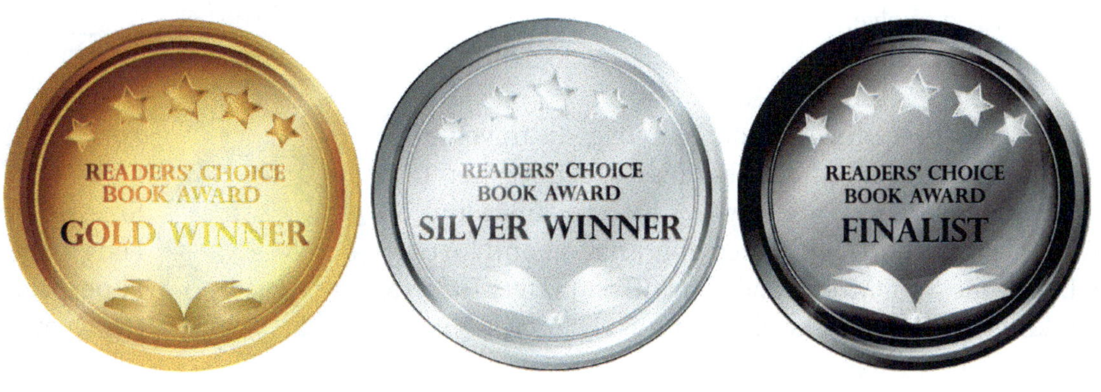

Children's Books

Spotlight Titles

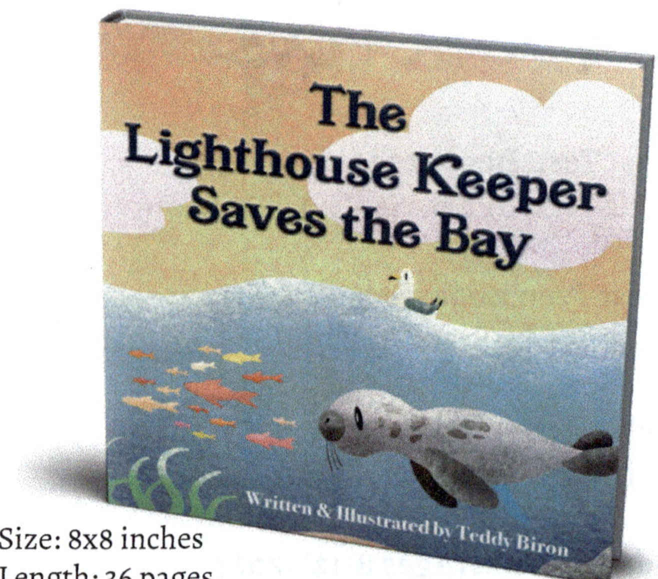

Size: 8x8 inches
Length: 36 pages
Paperback: $16.95 ISBN: 978-1954819658
Hardcover: $24.95 ISBN: 978-1954819542

The Lighthouse Keeper Saves the Bay
Written & Illustrated by Teddy Biron

Each morning, the lighthouse keeper awakes to watch seals play, fish swim, and seagulls fly. In his small, seaside town, the marine life lives in perfect harmony. One night while the lighthouse keeper sleeps, trouble lurks in the bay. The lighthouse keeper must work quickly to save the sea animals and find some help along the way.

About the Author
Theodore "Teddy" Biron is an award-winning artist from Cape Cod, Massachusetts. He graduated from Sandwich High School in 2020. He debuted his art for the first time at Reverdy Gallery in December of 2019. Living by the ocean has fueled his creativity and inspired most of his paintings and writings.

Alijah XII
by Kirja Ilijah

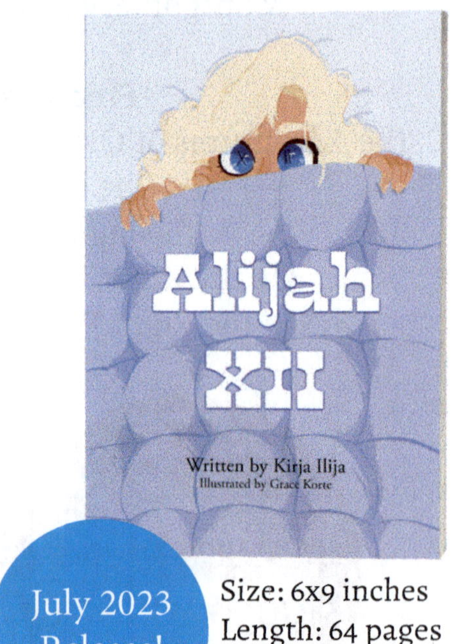

Wisdom passed down from generation to generation is a priceless jewel. On Alijah's twelfth birthday, this is no exception. During an outdoor adventure with her loving grandmother, Meema, Alijah learns valuable life lessons that help her prepare for young adulthood. No longer a child, but not quite a teenager, Alijah embraces the new beginning and responsibilities that come with turning twelve.

About the Author
Kirja Ilija lives in beautiful Arizona. She loves to travel, both domestically and abroad, largely because she does her best story brainstorming and plotting while out and about and on the move! An RV fanatic with a deep appreciation and love for Mother Earth, the Sun, Moon, and stars, Kirja prefers to write for the children around and the child within each one of us.

July 2023 Release!

Size: 6x9 inches
Length: 64 pages
Paperback: $12.99
ISBN: 978-1954819849

The Adventures of Owen & the Anthem Singer
by Todd Angilly & Rachel Goguen

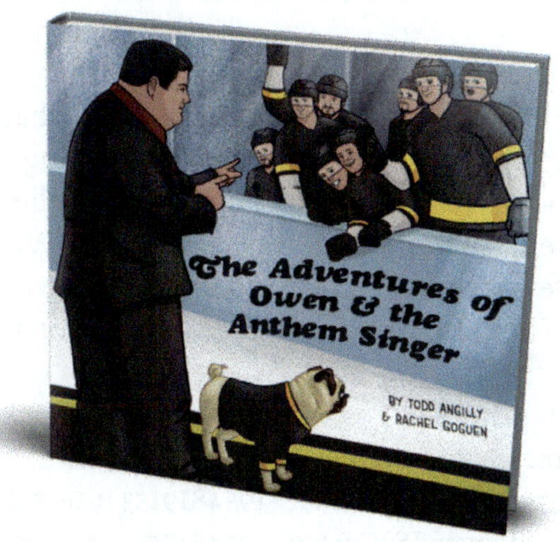

Join Boston Anthem Singer, Todd Angilly, and his best friend, Owen the Pug, as they embark on a hockey-filled adventure. Parents, children, hockey fans, and dog lovers will adore this endearing story that teaches the importance of friendship, hard work, and big dreams! *A portion of the profits from sales of this book will benefit the Boston Bruins Foundation.*

Length: 34 pages
Size: 8x8 inches
Paperback ISBN: 978-1954819351 ($16.95)
Hardcover ISBN: 978-1954819344 ($24.95)

Nate & His Magic Lion
by LaTonya Pinkard

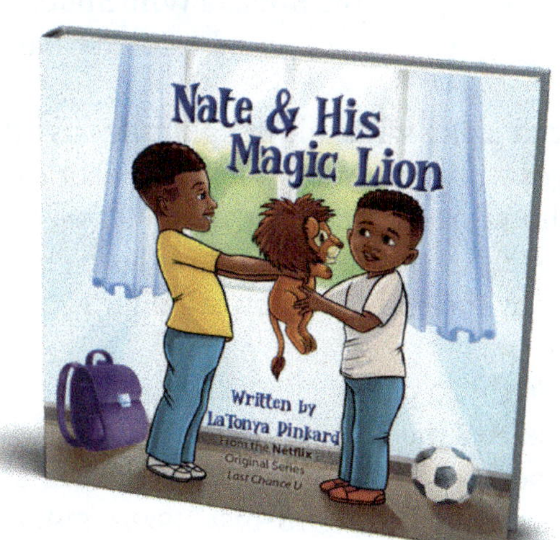

From LaTonya Pinkard of the Netflix Emmy award-winning series "Last Chance U" comes the exciting tale of Achi the Magic Lion!

Hi, everyone, I'm Nate! I'm afraid of the dark, but I want to be brave like my brother Mike. Come with me, and let's learn how to conquer our fears with help from my special friend, Achi the Magic Lion!

Length: 38 pages
Size: 8x8 inches
Paperback ISBN: 978-1954819320 ($16.95)
Hardcover ISBN: 978-1954819313 ($24.95)

The Falling Star Repairman
by Candido Bretto

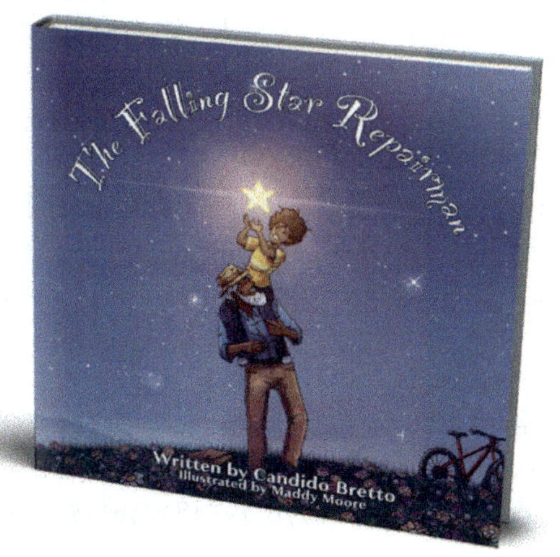

When stars fall from the sky, where do they land?
Do they get hurt?
Can they be fixed?
Join Elmer, the last falling-star repairman in the galaxy, as he tries to keep the night sky filled with starlight while making special friends along the way.

Length: 36 pages
Size: 8x8 inches
Paperback ISBN: 978-1954819641 ($16.95)
Hardcover ISBN: 978-1954819467 ($24.95)

There Are All Kinds of Bullies so What's a Kid to Do?
by Julie Hernandez

What is a Bully? Bullies come in all shapes and sizes, and they can be scary. What is important is learning how to deal with them. This book teaches kids how to deal with bullies through lessons, different scenarios, and interactive questions. Written by author and certified life coach, Julie Hernandez, There Are All Kinds of Bullies so What's a Kid to Do? teaches a necessary lesson to today's young generation.

Length: 36 pages
Size: 8x8 inches
Paperback ISBN: 978-1954819153 ($16.95)
Hardcover ISBN: 978-1954819016 ($24.95)

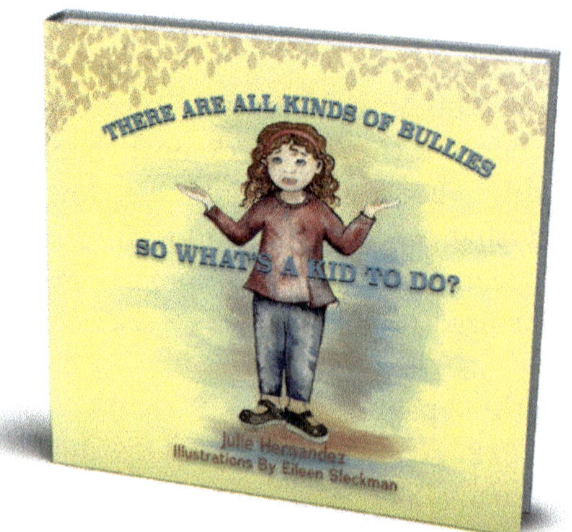

The Spooks Who Spooked Halloween
by David Charam

Read along with this delightfully frightful poem that children of all ages will appreciate. Kids will feel brave in the face of silly monsters who all want different amounts of candy. Parents will enjoy the lessons in subtraction as kids keep track of how much candy will be left by the end of Halloween night!

Length: 20 pages
Size: 8x8 inches
Paperback ISBN: 978-1954819290 ($12.95)
Hardcover ISBN: 978-1954819283 ($19.95)

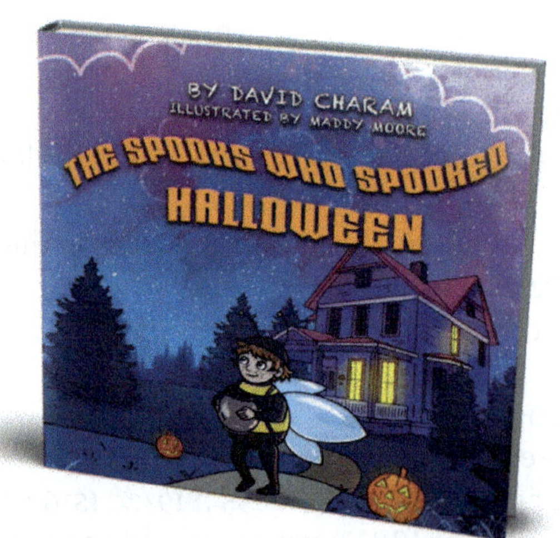

A Little Piece of the Big Picture
by Nicki MacKinnon

Parents are so smart! How do they know everything?!

Join Jameson as he learns about the little pieces of knowledge that help create "the big picture." Parents and teachers will love this book, which encourages children to get excited to learn new things!

Length: 20 pages
Size: 8x8 inches
Paperback ISBN: 978-1954819726 ($12.95)
Hardcover ISBN: 978-1954819481 ($19.95)

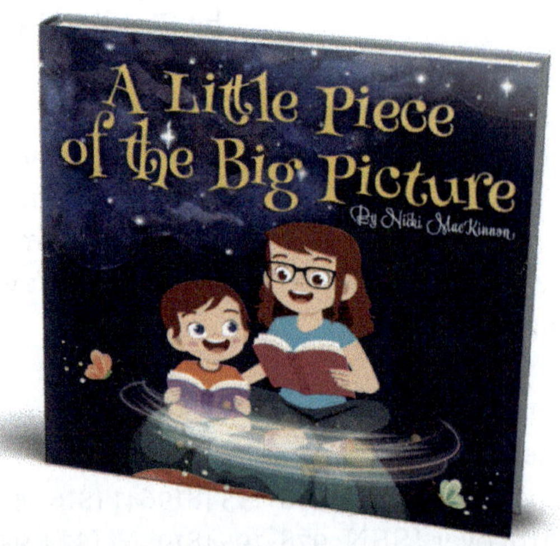

Trumpet the Miracle Wolf Pup
by Leokadia George

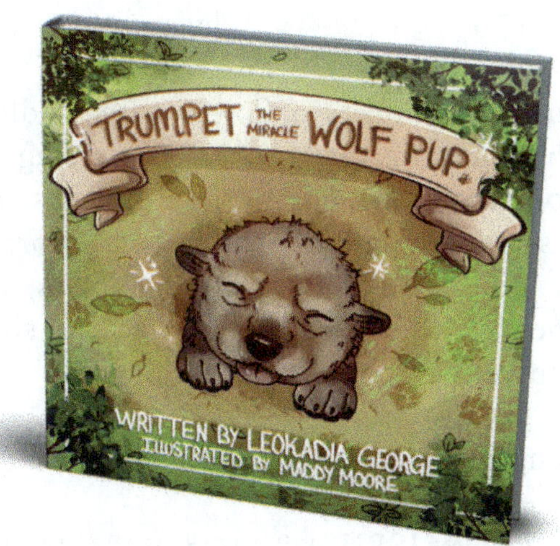

Based on true events surrounding the miraculous birth of one wolf pup at the Wolf Conservation Center, this book will fill your whole family with hope, while starting a conversation with your kids about the importance of saving endangered species.

Length: 40 pages
Size: 8x8 inches
Paperback ISBN: 978-1954819597 ($16.95)
Hardcover ISBN: 978-1954819238 ($24.95)

Trumpet the Miracle Wolf Pup: Trumpet Grows Up
by Leokadia George

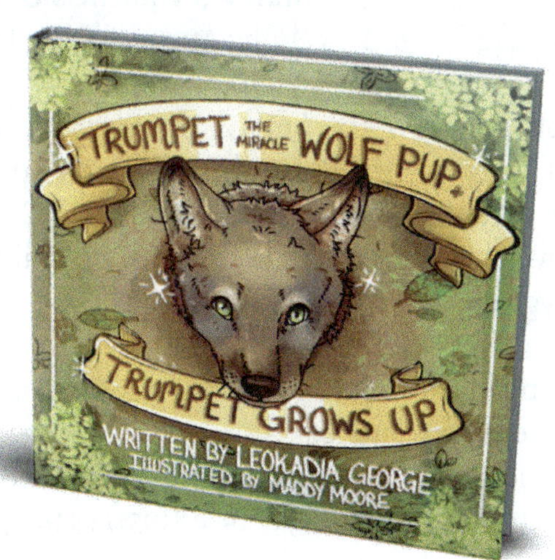

At the Wolf Conservation Center in New York, Trumpet the Miracle Wolf Pup is beginning to grow up. Join Trumpet as she explores the world around her-the sights, the smells, the sounds-and learns some valuable lessons along the way.

Length: 46 pages
Size: 8x8 inches
Paperback ISBN: 978-1954819603 ($16.95)
Hardcover ISBN: 978-1954819474 ($24.95)

Trumpet the Miracle Wolf Pup: Trumpet Finds Love
by Leokadia George

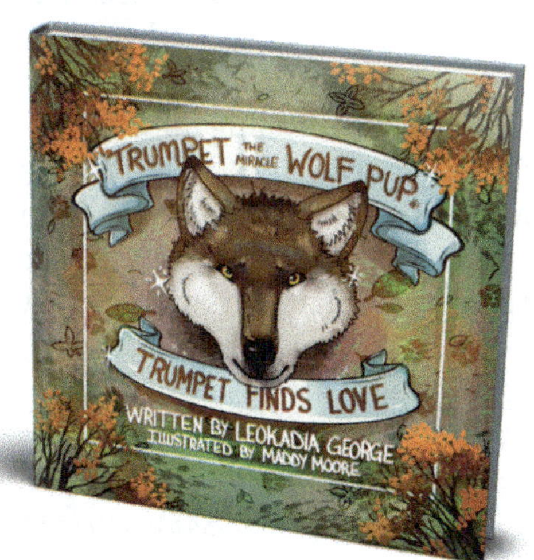

At the Wolf Conservation Center in New York, Trumpet the Miracle Wolf Pup is close to becoming an adult. After leaving the comfort of her family, she is relocated to a new home where she meets a special wolf named Lighthawk. Join Trumpet as she explores her new surroundings and meets her true love!

Sept. 2023 Release!

Length: 36 pages
Size: 8x8 inches
Paperback ISBN: 978-1961978010 ($16.95)
Hardcover ISBN: 978-1954819900 ($24.95)

I Love Dandelions
by August E. Allen

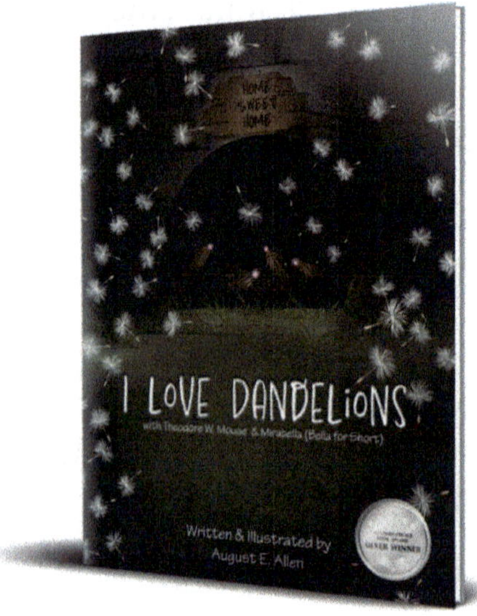

The dandelion is a flower with wildlife superpowers, providing abundant nectar and pollen, giving food to a wide range of pollinators such as bees, butterflies, moths, fireflies, and other insects. Dandelion seeds and leaves provide food for a wide variety of wildlife, including birds, rabbits, deer, and even bears! Join Theodore W. Mouse as he and his siblings uncover the magical superpowers of dandelions!

Length: 34 pages
Size: 8.5x11 inches
Hardcover ISBN: 978-1954819528 ($24.95)

Maizy & Charlie's GERM BOOK
by Annie & Gilly DeCosta

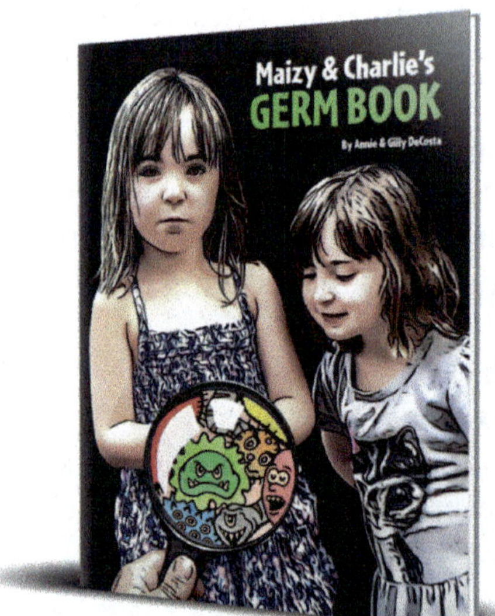

Join sisters Maizy and Charlie as they teach young readers to be wary of scary germs! From the ways kids can prevent the spread of germs to where germs can live, Maizy and Charlie cover it all. Parents will love this book, which encourages children to prioritize health and hygiene.

Length: 36 pages
Size: 8.5x11 inches
Paperback ISBN: 978-1954819771 ($16.95)
Hardcover ISBN: 978-1954819511 ($24.95)

Lessons Learned from Atka
by Lois Kral

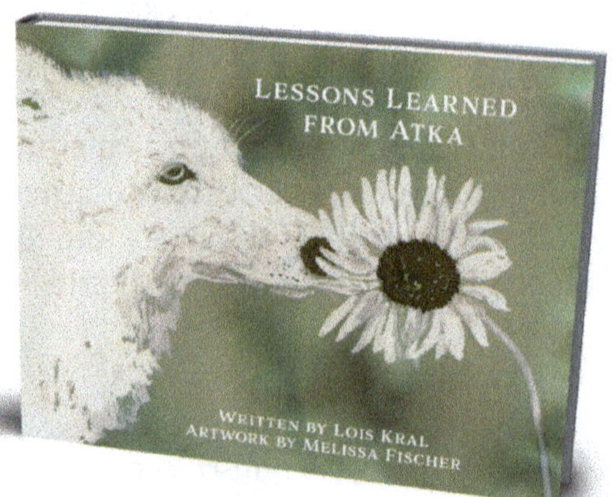

Atka was the traveling ambassador for the Wolf Conservation Center in South Salem, New York. This special wolf was known not only regionally, but also nationally and globally. The lessons learned from his life will inspire hope, acceptance, and positive change in the lives of animal lovers across the world.

Length: 32 pages
Size: 11x8.5 inches
Paperback ISBN: 978-1954819610 ($16.95)
Hardcover ISBN: 978-1954819429 ($24.95)

The Colors Inside of Me
by AmyLee Westervelt

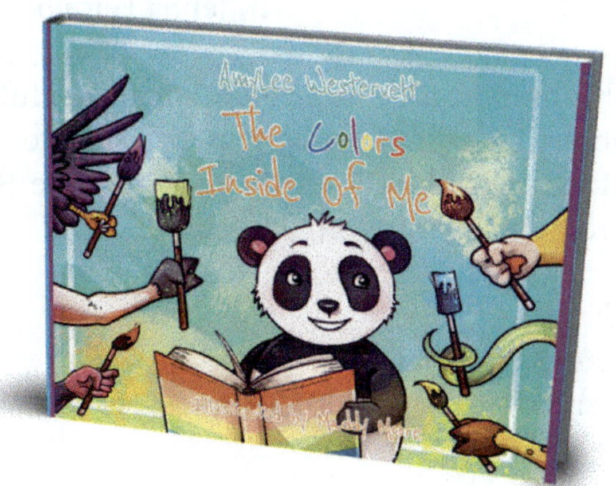

Panda is excited for a new art project, but he gets discouraged when it has to do with finding his inner beauty. With some help from his teacher and classmates, he realizes the colors he thought were missing were inside of him all along.

Length: 48 pages
Size: 11x8.5 inches
Hardcover ISBN: 978-1954819221 ($24.95)

Crabby Cakes
by Eileen Clancy-Pantano

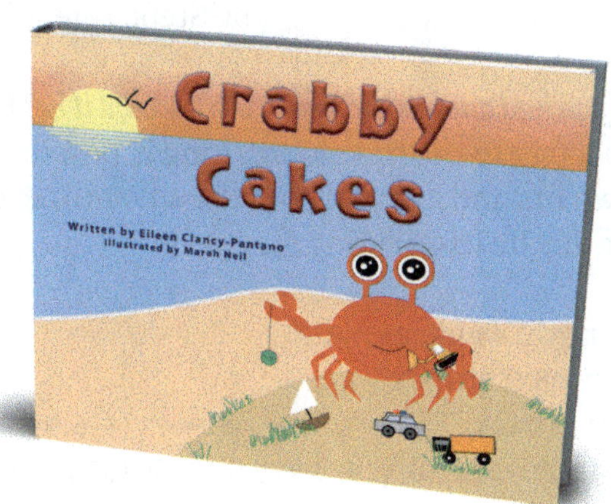

Crabby Cakes would rather spend time with his toy boats, trucks, and tractors than his friends or family. He believes things, things, and more things will lead to happiness. With the help of his mother and a concerned friend, Crabby learns that filling his life with people who care about him is more important than having all the toys in the world.

Length: 20 pages
Size: 11x8.5 inches
Hardcover ISBN: 978-1954819795 ($19.95)

Finn Finally Seas
by Eileen Clancy-Pantano

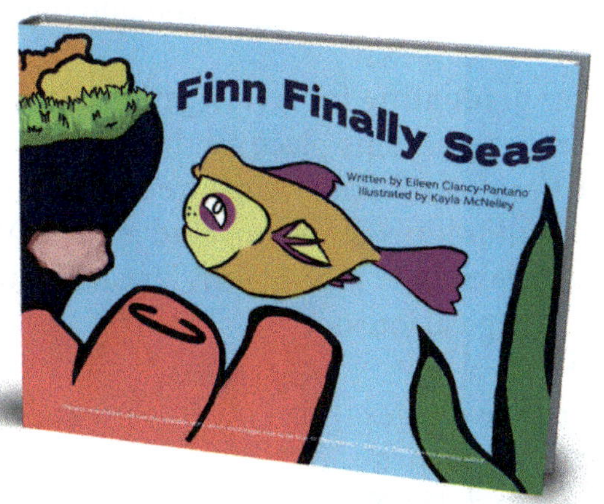

Why would you want to be anyone else but you?

Finn wants to fit in with the other fish in his school, but because of his unusual features, he always seems to stand out. On a journey towards self-acceptance, he learns a valuable lesson about his special place in the world.

Length: 32 pages
Size: 11x8.5 inches
Hardcover ISBN: 978-1954819573 ($24.95)

The Baby Cow
by Jenna Feitelberg

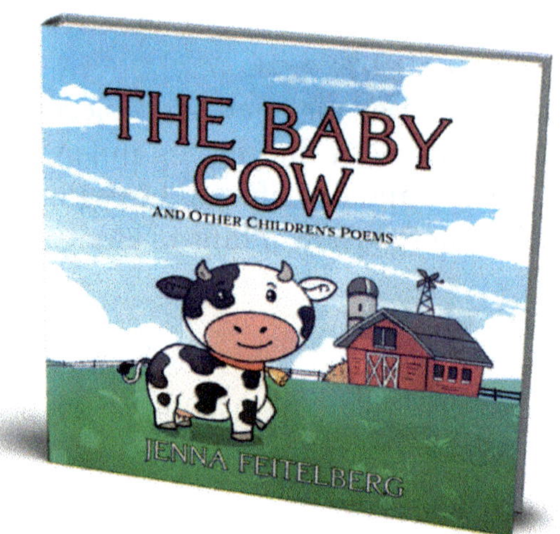

This humorous, educational, and beautifully illustrated collection of poetry by Jenna Feitelberg includes the following poems: The Puppy, Monster in the Closet, Baby Sister, The Baby Cow, Blueberry, The Tree, and Swing from the Moon.

Length: 52 pages
Size: 8x8 inches
Hardcover ISBN: 978-1954819214 ($24.95)

My One Wish
by Stephanie Ade

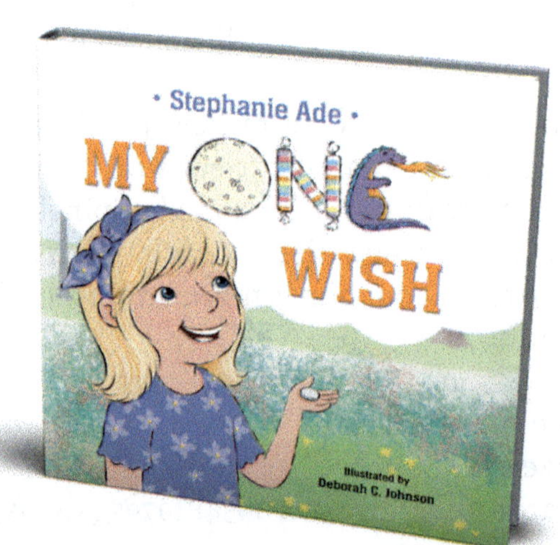

If you had one wish to make, what would it be? From a room full of puppies to a trip to the moon, anything is possible with a little imagination! Parents and kids will love the adventures that lie between the covers of this heartwarming story.

Length: 44 pages
Size: 8x8 inches
Paperback ISBN: 978-1954819672 ($16.95)
Hardcover ISBN: 978-1954819566 ($24.95)

The Cam-Mac Adventure Express
by Stephanie L. Brazer

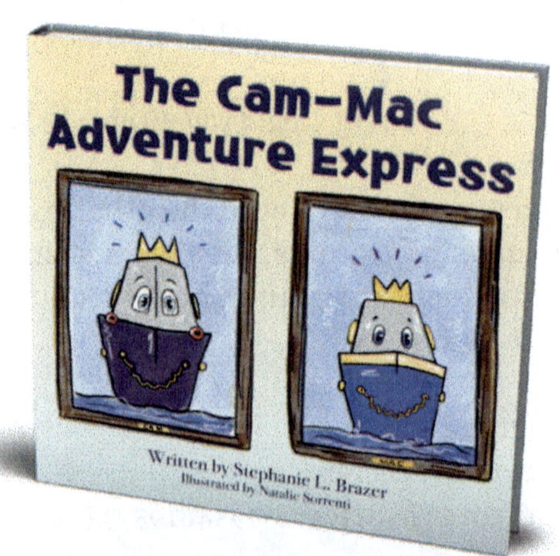

After graduating from Navigation Class, Cam sets sail from Boston Harbor to find his place on the high seas. After a dizzying tango in the Bermuda Triangle and an encounter with a couple of other ships, Cam finds himself on a royal adventure. With a BIG imagination and some help from his brother, Mac, Cam takes the Royals of Concord on a magical journey.

Length: 44 pages
Size: 8x8 inches
Paperback ISBN: 978-1954819559 ($16.95)
Hardcover ISBN: 978-1954819535 ($24.95)

One the Right Path: Book One
by Brett Gunning & Stacy Padula

Join Jayden, Jordan, their little sister Jasmine, and their friend Shai as the group experiences their first basketball camp and learns lessons about life along the way. Parents will love this uplifting book, which encourages children to love others and teaches the importance of making people feel welcome and loved.

Length: 24 pages
Size: 8x8 inches
Paperback ISBN: 978-1954819078 ($16.95)
Hardcover ISBN: 978-1954819030 ($24.95)

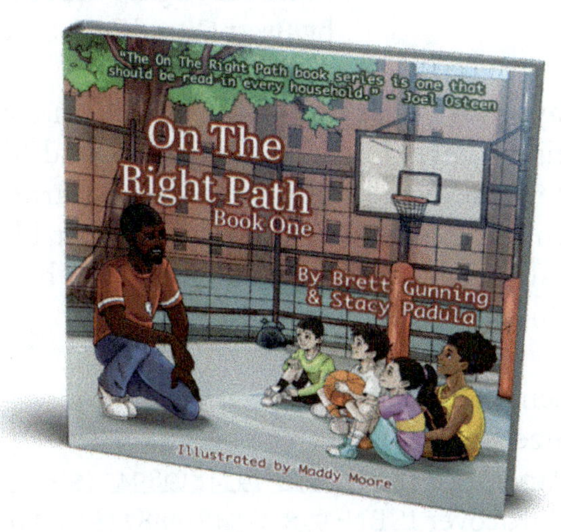

One the Right Path: Book Two
by Brett Gunning & Stacy Padula

Jordan is at his second day of basketball camp with his brother Jayden and his sister Jasmine. Along with new basketball skills, the kids are learning life-lessons such as how to be unselfish. Just like the other On The Right Path books, this is sure to become a beloved story for parents and children alike.

Length: 24 pages
Size: 8x8 inches
Paperback ISBN: 978-1954819276 ($16.95)
Hardcover ISBN: 978-1954819269 ($24.95)

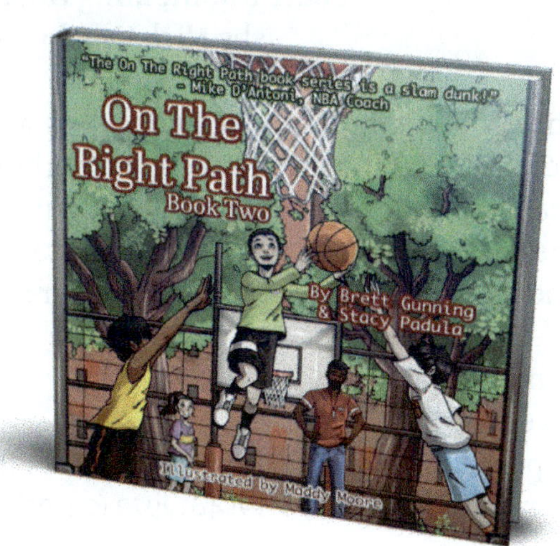

One the Right Path: Book Three
by Brett Gunning & Stacy Padula

Shai is at his third day of basketball camp with his friends Jayden, Jordan, and Jasmine. Along with new basketball skills, the kids are learning life-lessons such as the importance of eating healthy and growing strong. Just like the other On the Right Path books, this is sure to become a beloved story for parents and children alike.

Length: 24 pages
Size: 8x8 inches
Paperback ISBN: 978-1954819405 ($16.95)
Hardcover ISBN: 978-1954819412 ($24.95)

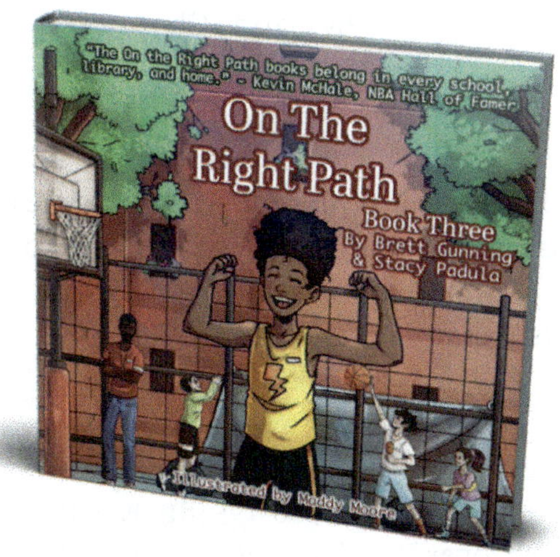

One the Right Path: Book Four
by Brett Gunning & Stacy Padula

Jayden has just completed his fourth day of basketball camp with his siblings, Jordan and Jasmine, and his friend Shai. Along with new basketball skills, the kids are learning life-lessons such as the importance of forgiving others. Just like the other On the Right Path books, this is sure to become a beloved story for parents and children alike.

Length: 24 pages
Size: 8x8 inches
Paperback ISBN: 978-19548198945 ($16.95)
Hardcover ISBN: 978-1954819887 ($24.95)

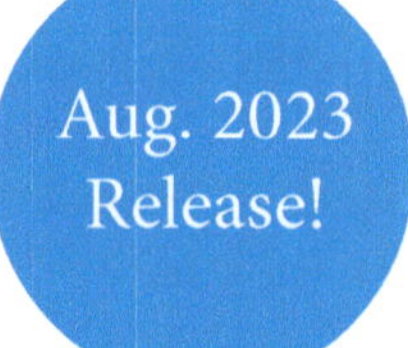

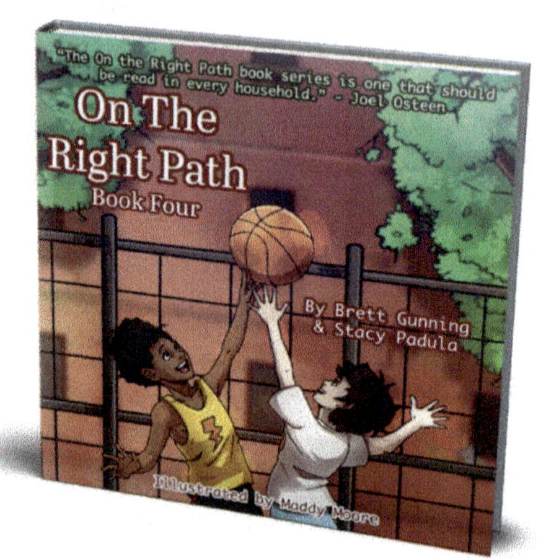

There's Something About ROBINS
by Nick Vakalopoulos

There's Something About ROBINS is a beautiful, poetic tribute to Robins with artwork derived from author Nick Vakalopoulos's many years as a wildlife photographer. An informative resource that takes the reader into the world of Robins and their daily activities, this book will be embraced by nature lovers and curious children alike.

Length: 48 pages
Size: 8.5x8.5 inches
Paperback ISBN: 978-1961978034 ($16.95)
Hardcover ISBN: 978-1954819979 (24.95)

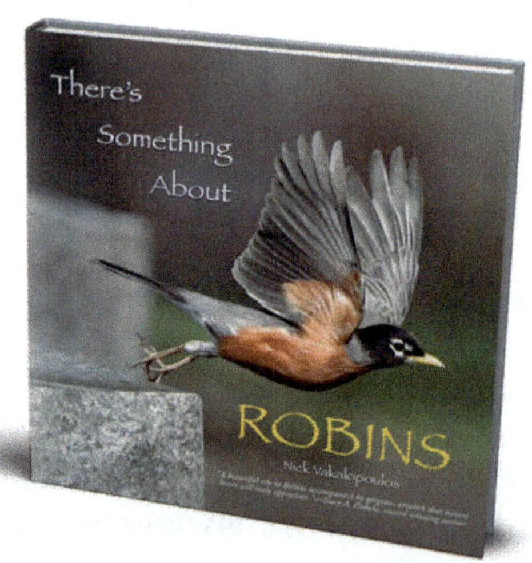

Nelson's Gadern
by Candy O'Terry & Colleen Esposito

Friendship Grows in Nelson's Garden

When sisters, Belle and Rosie, become enchanted by their neighbor's garden, a meaningful friendship is formed that spans generations. As flowers bloom and wishes come true, the girls learn a valuable lesson.

Length: 32 pages
Size: 11x8.5 inches
Paperback ISBN: 978-19548199936 ($16.95)
Hardcover ISBN: 978-19548199621 (24.95)

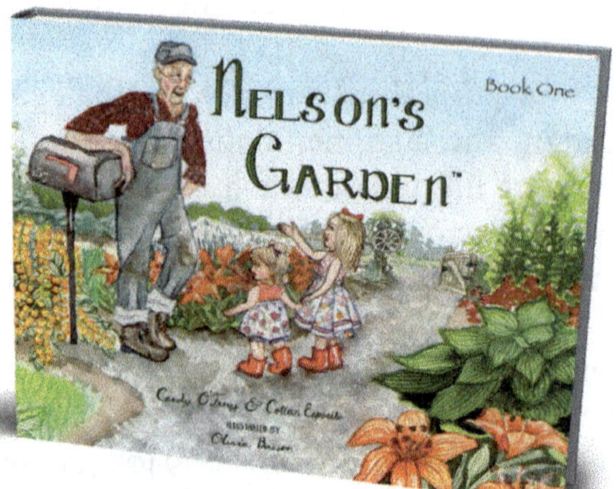

Errol: The Cat Who Wasn't a Cat
by Ross & Tonya Grifkin

Errol grew up believing he was a normal cat, and just like any normal cat, he went to college, got a job at a bank, and worked every day. When a gang of bandits try to rob Errol's bank, a dragon magically appears to save the day. Soon after, Errol learns his life is anything but normal and he is anything but a normal cat. He's not a cat at all! With a dangerous group of villains chasing after him, Errol must uncover the truth about his mythical origins.

Length: 80 pages (full color)
Size: 6x9 inches
Paperback ISBN: 978-1954819788 ($12.99)

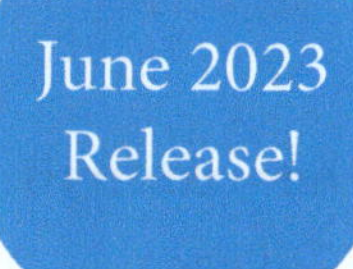

June 2023
Release!

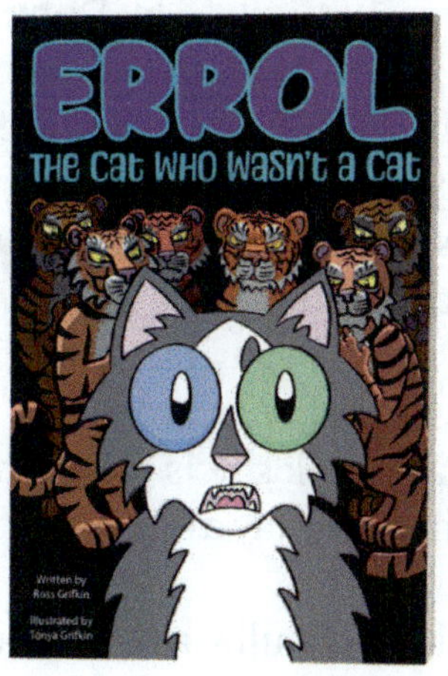

Bradykin Visits Martha's Vineyard
by Susan & Megan Downing

Join Bradykin and his family as they explore Martha's Vineyard on a fun-filled, summer vacation. From seeing the brightly colored Gingerbread Cottages to biking through Edgartown to sailing by South Beach, Bradykin's week on Martha's Vineyard is full of tradition and delight for all ages.

Length: 32 pages
Size: 8.5x11 inches
Paperback ISBN: 978-1954819870 ($16.95)
Hardcover ISBN: 978-1954819856 ($24.95)

July 2023
Release!

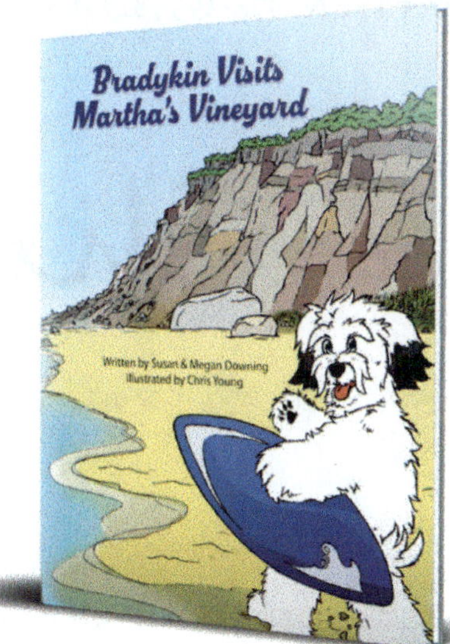

Bradykin's Joyful Adventure
by Susan & Megan Downing

Join Bradykin on a quest for smiles and happiness! From apple picking to sledding to building sandcastles and everything in between, Bradykin's joyful adventure is full of year-round delight for all ages.

Length: 30 pages
Size: 8.5x11 inches
Paperback ISBN: 978-1961978041 ($16.95)
Hardcover ISBN: 978-1961978003 ($24.95)

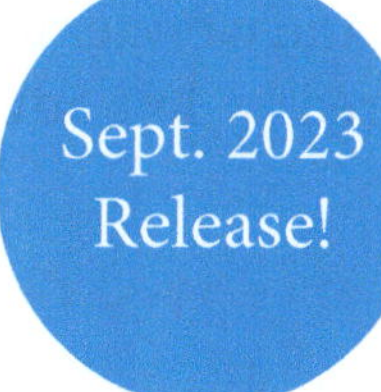

Sept. 2023
Release!

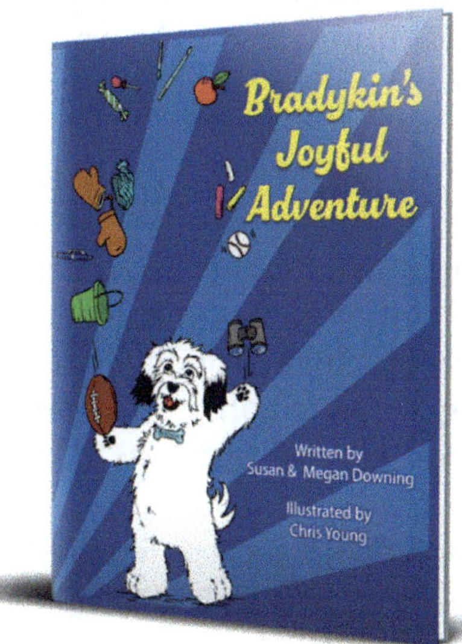

10% of publishing royalties are donated to animal rescues

Chili Chinchilla
by Donna MacLeod

Deep in the Andes Valley lives a chinchilla named Chili,
Unlike any you've seen before.
She wears a coat of argentine blue,
Too beautiful to ignore.
Although she is beautiful, sometimes she is sad,
For she is never invited to play.
The animals think she is far too different,
And laugh at her day after day.

Join Chili Chinchilla as she teaches the other animals valuable lessons about friendship, acceptance, and kindness.

Paperback ISBN: 978-1961978027 ($16.95)
Hardcover ISBN: 978-1954819986 ($24.95)

Length: 28 pages
Size: 8.5x11 inches

Christian Books
Spotlight Title

Seas the Day
by Dani Ruth Romero

Timmy Tortuga is a content little turtle until the day he gets bullied over his old bike. When Timmy begins to question why he can't have nice things like the other turtles, Mama takes him on an undersea adventure to help him "seas" the day. By seeing the beauty in God's blessings, Timmy learns the priceless joy that comes with thanking God for all he gives.

About the Author
Dani Ruth Romero is a self-taught artist from the USA with a mission of radiating life, color, and joy through her paintings and illustrations. Her vision for her artwork is to create whimsical products that stir a rekindling of childlike awe and wonder for adults of all ages. The majority of her work is inspired by her adventures traveling with God across the globe.

Paperback ISBN: 978-1954819832 ($16.95)
Hardcover: ISBN: 978-19548198252 ($24.95)

Length: 34 pages
Size: 8.5x11 inches

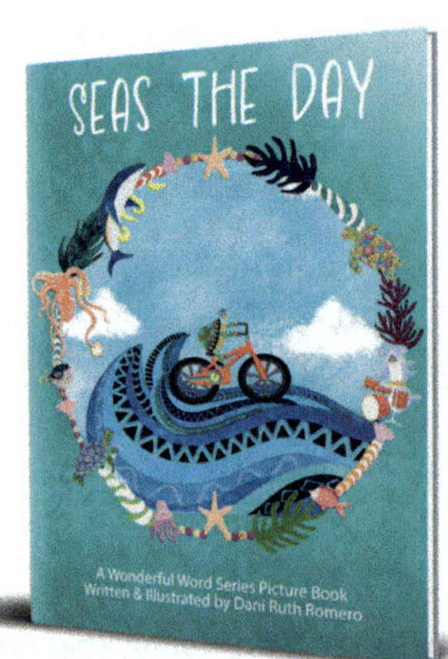

Seas the Day - Coloring Book Edition
by Dani Ruth Romero

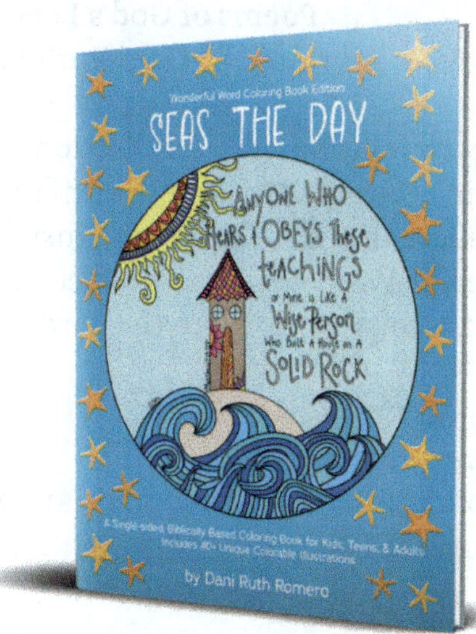

"Seas" the day with the Wonderful Word of God! This ocean-themed coloring book for kids, teens, and adults includes 40+ single-sided unique illustrations that celebrate God's nautical design and adorable sea creatures. All pages are inspired by scripture.

This coloring book is inspired by Dani R. Romero's Christian children's book, Seas the Day.

Length: 88 pages
Size: 8.5x11 inches
Paperback ISBN: 978-1954819818 ($9.99)

Poems of Praise & Wonder
by Dani Ruth Romero

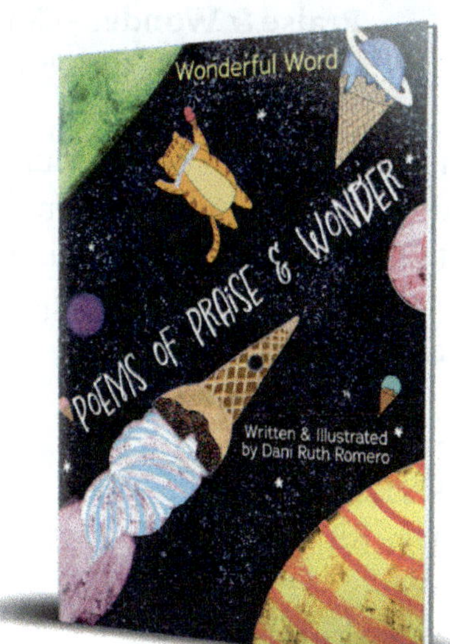

This collection of vibrantly illustrated poems uplifts and inspires readers as it celebrates the glorious characteristics of God. Perfect for both children and adults, Poems of Praise & Wonder incorporates the following themes: God's miraculous ways, God's gifts of hope and joy, God as our protector, the peace of God that surpasses all understanding, & God's promise of abundant life.

Length: 60 pages
Size: 8.5x11 inches
Paperback ISBN: 978-1954819634 ($18.95)
Hardcover ISBN: 978-1954819580 ($28.00)

Praise & Wonder - Coloring Book Edition
by Dani Ruth Romero

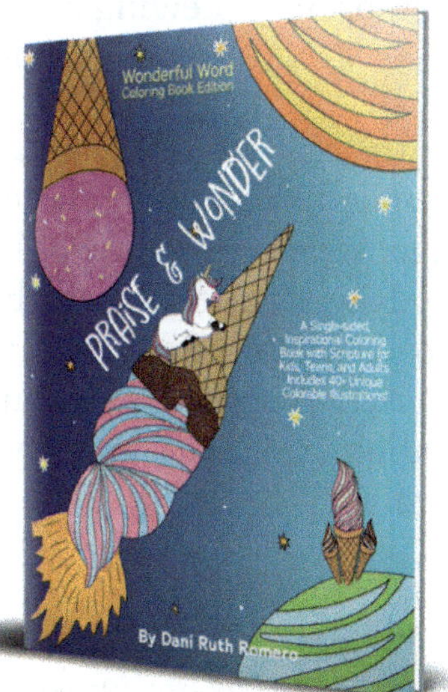

Deepen your walk with God through art! This coloring book for kids, teens, and adults includes 40+ single-sided unique illustrations that celebrate the glorious characteristics of God. All pages are inspired by scripture. The whimsical designs will be beloved by children and make adults feel childlike again. This coloring book is inspired by Dani R. Romero's poetry book, Poems of Praise & Wonder.

Length: 82 pages
Size: 8.5x11 inches
Paperback ISBN: 978-1954819627 ($9.99)

Poems of God's Loving Promises
by Dani Ruth Romero

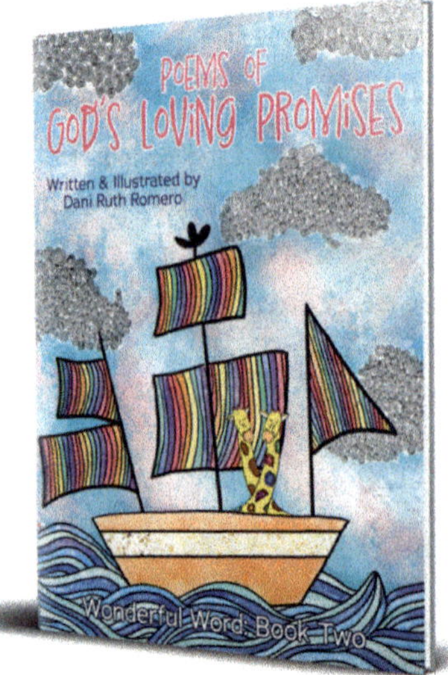

This beautifully illustrated collection of love-themed poems inspires adoration towards God for His unfailing love & promises for those who believe in Him. This second installment in Dani Ruth Romero's Wonderful Word series is perfect for children, teens, and adults who want to grow closer to the Lord.

Length: 56 pages
Size: 8.5x11 inches
Paperback ISBN: 978-1954819757 ($18.95)
Hardcover ISBN: 978-1954819733 ($28.00)

Praise & Wonder - Coloring Book Edition
by Dani Ruth Romero

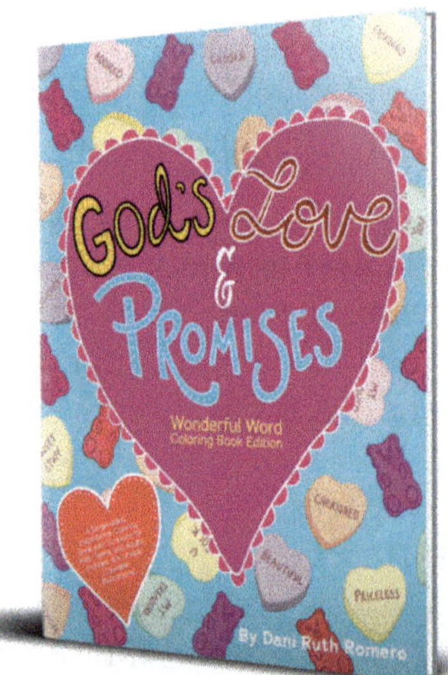

Deepen your walk with God through art! This coloring book for kids, teens, and adults includes 40+ single-sided unique illustrations that celebrate the glorious characteristics of God. All pages are inspired by scripture. The whimsical designs will be beloved by children and make adults feel childlike again.

Length: 100 pages
Size: 8.5x11 inches
Paperback ISBN: 978-1954819740 ($11.99)

Mosaic: Renewing Your Mental Health With God
by Cameron Pace

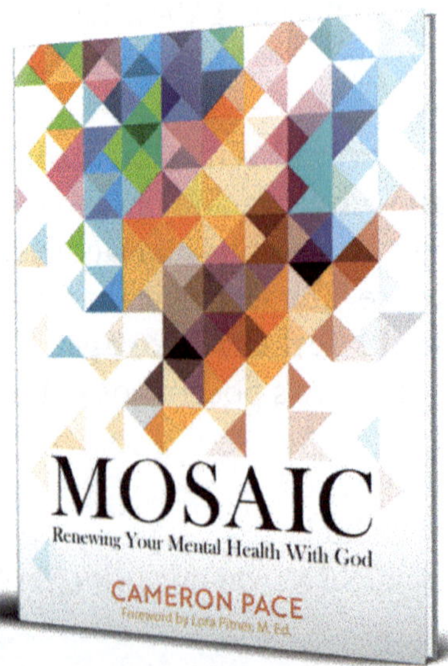

Can you struggle with mental health and still be a Christian? Yes. There is a stigma often found in churches that gives birth to the lie that you cannot struggle with mental health and still be a Christian. This Bible study was created to combat that lie with the truth that God wants to guide you through the healing process. Mosaic focuses on the intersection of faith and mental health, along with the ways the combination of spiritual and psychological practices can help bring about healing.

Length: 90 pages
Size: 8.5x11 inches
Paperback ISBN: 978-1954819696 ($16.95)

All In: For Those in Search of Something More
by Adam Palmer

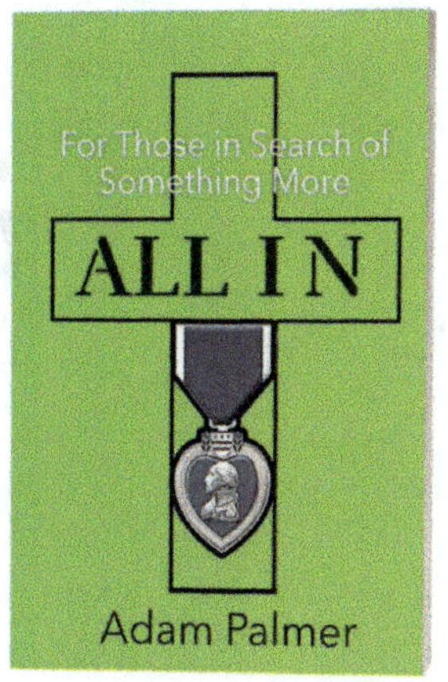

US Army Veteran Adam Palmer's memoir offers a gut-wrenching expose' of his desert conversion and his mission to share the Gospel in 48 days, in 48 states to reach 1 million people. For combat veterans and everyday readers alike, ALL IN was written to help others find their identity and purpose in serving Christ and others.

Length: 158 pages
Size: 6x9 inches
Paperback ISBN: 978-1954819139 ($14.99)

My Refuge: Finding Peace & Strength in Uncertainty
by Debra Fredette

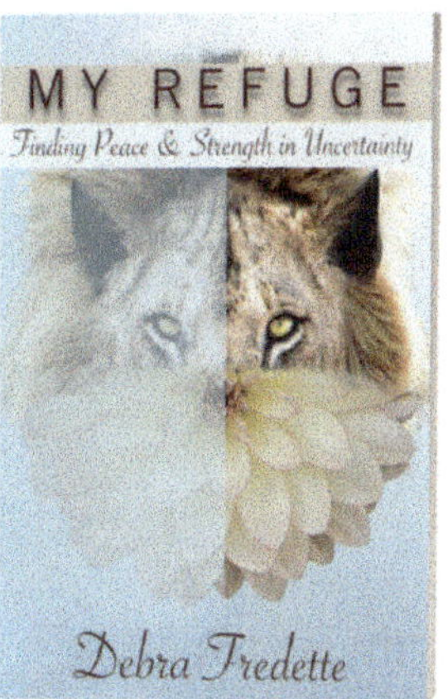

In a world of chaos and devastation, how do people find serenity and security? In My Refuge, Debra Fredette shares how she dealt with similar circumstances and found peace and strength in a time of unrest. This materialized when she decided to travel to Africa in 2014 to help relieve the oppression of deaf children. Join Deb as she shares her secrets on how to fight hate with love, advance when you are afraid, and persevere even when you are growing weary.

Length: 56 pages
Size: 6x9 inches
Paperback ISBN: 978-1954819757 ($9.99)

Persevering Through Seasons of Despair
by Debra Fredette

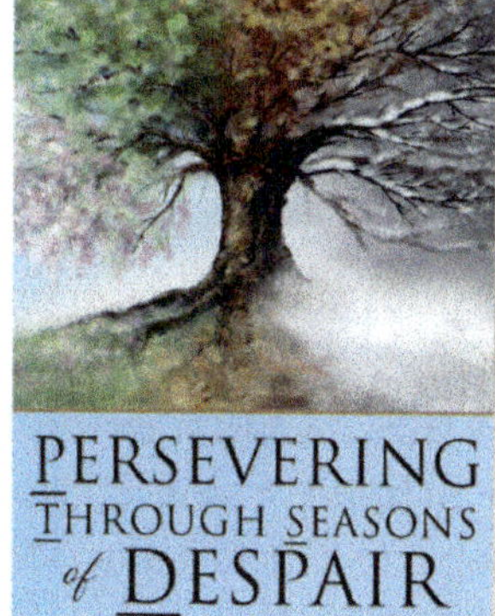

If you are tired of always being on the defense and running for shelter when winds of anxiety, fear, and depression attack, then this book is for you. To defeat any enemy, you must know your enemy's tactics and have the right weapons of destruction. PERSEVERING THROUGH SEASONS OF DESPAIR will not only reveal the forces behind despair, anxiety, and depression, but also teach you how to annihilate them.

Oct. 2023 Release!

Length: 300 pages
Size: 6x9 inches
Paperback ISBN: 978-1-961978058 ($18.95)

10% of publishing royalties are donated to animal rescues

Fiction Books

Spotlight Title

Between Heaven & 42nd and Broadway
by Michael Caissie

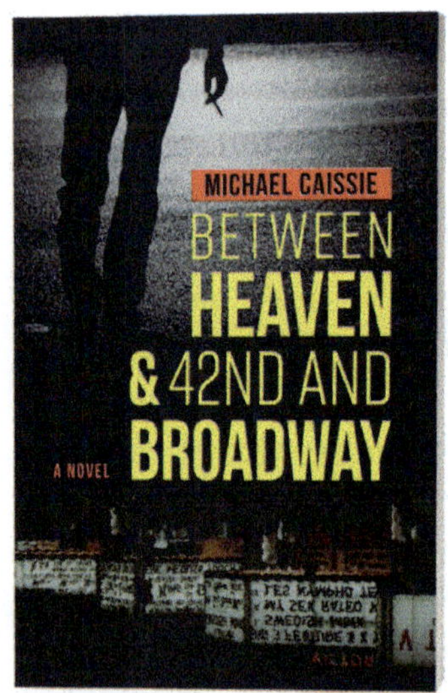

Size: 6x9 inches
Length: 142 pages

A shadow of a being, war veteran Paul Stevenson moves through New York City without purpose. When the blood spatter from a fellow subway rider and thousands of dollars' worth of cocaine fall to Paul's feet, he is forced to open his eyes to a new reality: the world of sex, crime, and drugs that is 1970's Manhattan—the life in which Paul has suddenly become a main character. *Is there any light in the future of the Big Apple? Or will Paul succumb to the dark shadow of organized crime that encamps the greatest city in the world?*

About the Author

Born and raised in Massachusetts, Michael Caissie studied business at Boston College before moving to California to pursue screenwriting and directing, where he has written and directed such films as NO TEARS IN HELL and HUNTER'S MOON, which he also produced. Michael also wrote THE DEVIL'S TRAP, starring Bruce Dern, and co-wrote HANGMAN, starring Al Pacino, Karl Urban, and Brittany Snow. In 2020 he wrote the Mexican film, SIN ORIGEN, for famed horror director, Rigoberto Castaneda. Most recently he was the co-writer for the soon-to-be-released action film THE ISLAND, starring Michael Jai White.

Paperback: $14.99 ISBN: 978-1954819764

Course Correction
by Richard Cutler

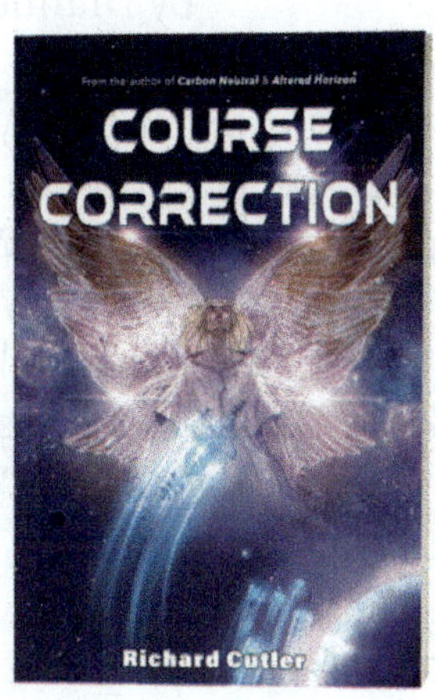

The year is 2085, and a fleet of interstellar ships hurtles toward a solar system that is hoped will offer a new home for humanity. Setting up a wormhole gate on one of Epsilon Eridani's planets would provide an escape for the billions left on an overpopulated and resource-poor Earth. Humanity has leaped into the stars, but will this be our future-or a last desperate act before extinction?

Length: 274 pages
Size: 6x9 inches
Paperback ISBN: 978-1954819436 ($18.95)

Carbon Neutral
by Richard Cutler

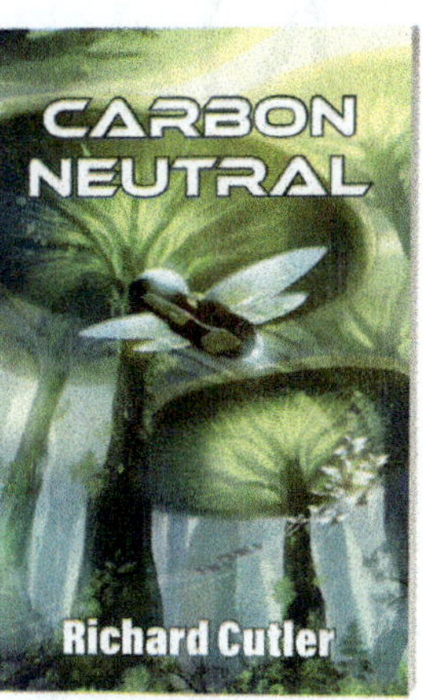

After a successful space mission on a fleet of Star Ships, Earth's best and brightest minds return to find their planet ravaged by a viral catastrophe. Without leadership or direction, the loosely reorganized United Nations Stellar Commission sits in a state of stagnation. The newly appointed commissioners of the UNSC must decide whether or not to risk the four functional Star Ships that remain in the hope of discovering another inhabitable planet.

Length: 284 pages
Size: 6x9 inches
Paperback ISBN: 978-1954819009 ($18.95)

Altered Horizon
by Richard Cutler

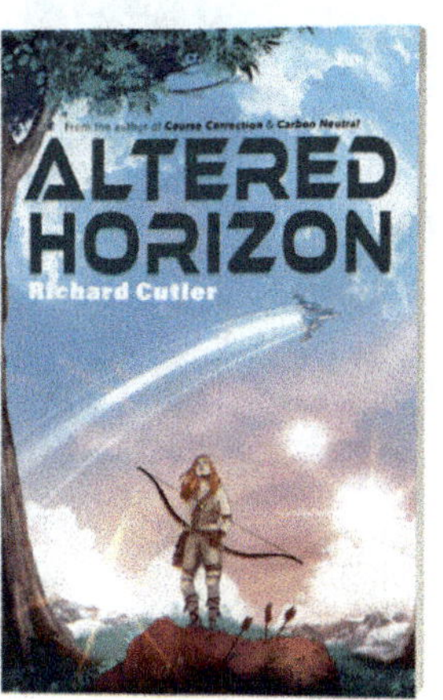

After early successes, ongoing problems on Earth have kept the Star Ship Fleet in a holding pattern awaiting further instructions. Then, in 2147, the United Nations Stellar Commission decides to launch a series of new and exciting missions with the primary goal of setting up a colony and wormhole gate on one of the planets orbiting Alpha Centauri.

Length: 282 pages
Size: 6x9 inches
Paperback ISBN: 978-1954819368 ($18.95)

Mystery at Chilmark
by Dianne Hunt Smith

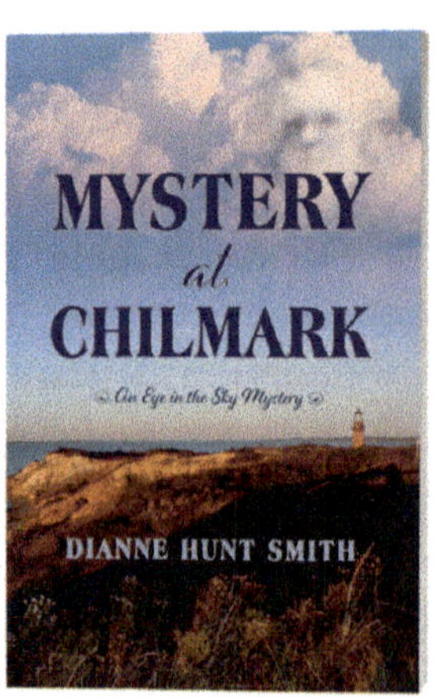

Kat MacIntyre knows her family isn't like most others—but neither is she. She has special gifts that she rarely speaks about, gifts most people would not understand. When a work assignment brings Kat and her rescue dog, Dash, to Martha's Vineyard, she finally gets a chance to investigate her family's puzzling history, including the strange tale of a lost fortune. As supernatural occurrences abound, Kat inches closer to solving the Vineyard's greatest mystery of all.

Length: 96 pages
Size: 6x9 inches
Paperback ISBN: 978-1954819801 ($12.99)

Non-fiction Books

Spotlight Title

The Original: Living Life Through Hockey
by Norm Beaudin with Kim Passante

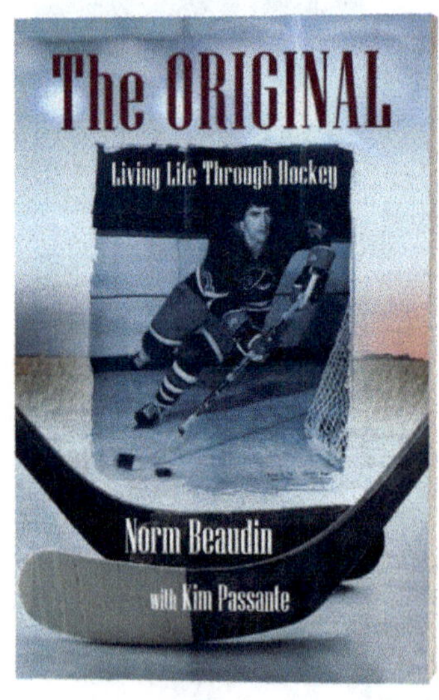

Canadian former professional hockey player Norm Beaudin is best known for being "The Original Jet"—the first to sign with the Winnipeg Jets Franchise in 1972. He played twenty-five games in the National Hockey League (NHL) and 335 games in the World Hockey Association (WHA). Beaudin also played for the Minnesota North Stars and the St. Louis Blues. In The Original, Beaudin shares his chaotic life of over fifty years-from his $2 makeshift Zamboni job as a boy to the success of earning the title of a professional hockey player.

About the Author
Kim Passante has known Norm Beaudin since he first moved to Arizona. She is a lifelong sports enthusiast, who grew up in a family of motorsports drivers. It was a natural fit for her to dive into Norm's world of hockey and pen his inspiring story. Over the years, she has written everything from poetry to marketing literature to legal case preparation. Kim resides with her family in beautiful and sunny Scottsdale, Arizona.

Size: 6x9 inches
Length: 172 pages
Hardcover ISBN: 978-1954819337 ($24.95)
Paperback ISBN: 978-1954819498 ($16.95)

Mexico Got Lucky
by Rico Austin

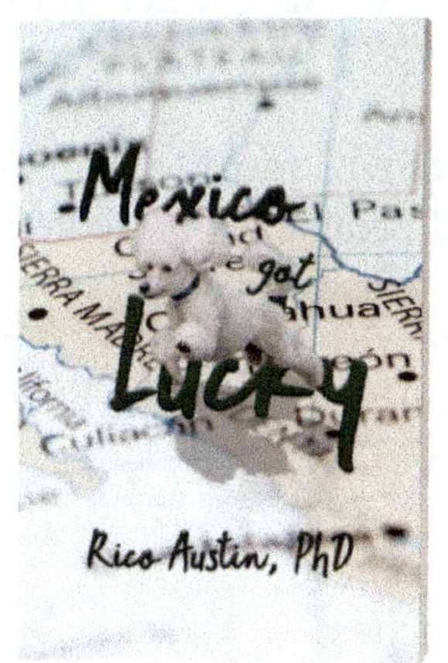

Mexico Got Lucky shares the true, epic story of how the State of Sonora, Mexico and communities of San Carlos, Guaymas, Hermosillo, Empalme and Obregon came together to try to locate Lucky's captors, free Lucky from harms way, and get him into Jim Kawaguchi's arms. Mexicans, Americans, Canadians, and the Consulate of Hermosillo joined forces in an attempt to solve the greatest mystery of dog theft in Mexico's history.

Length: 182 pages
Size: 6x9 inches
Paperback ISBN: 978-1954819399 ($16.95)

The Monster: Helping Families Navigate Addiction
by Julie Hernandez

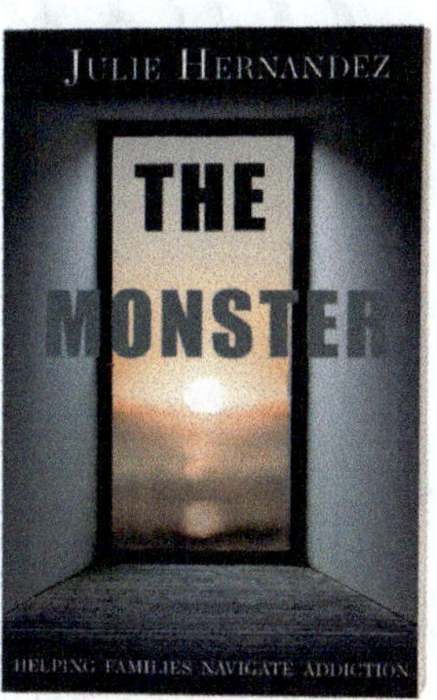

The Monster is a guide for those who have a loved one struggling with addiction. This work has already been used in support groups and with individual families around the country. The hidden battle in addiction is often the one fought by the family members who suffer along with the addict. This book shows them how they can help themselves and their loved ones escape from "the monster" of addiction.

Length: 30 pages (full color)
Size: 5x8 inches
Paperback ISBN: 978-1954819023 ($12.99)

Here's Why You Can't Find Love
by Ted Santos

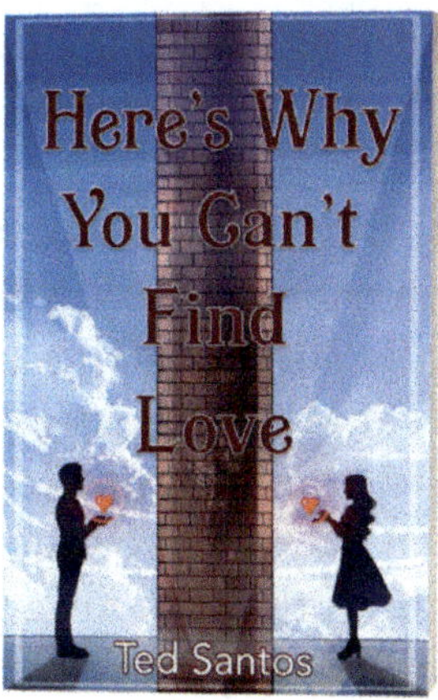

Whether he is coaching CEOs of midsize to large companies looking to create a breakthrough or advising individuals on how to have successful partnerships, Ted Santos uses his understanding of human behavior. Here's Why You Can't Find Love will help you discover counter-intuitive approaches to creating interpersonal breakthroughs in love, work, and play.

Length: 108 pages
Size: 6x9 inches
Paperback ISBN: 978-1954819610 ($12.99)

10% of publishing royalties are donated to animal rescues

When Did I Become the Dumpster?
Raising & Teaching Rebellious Teenagers
by Joanne Colombini

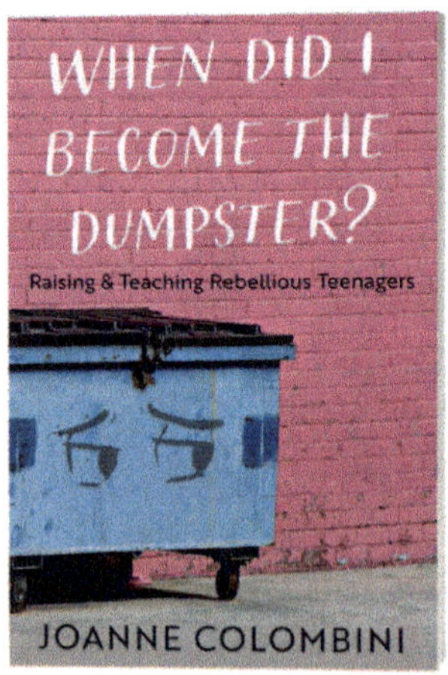

Most adults will admit, it can be a struggle to deal with teenagers. *When Did I Become the Dumpster?* gives readers an inside look at the challenges of motherhood, as well as what it means to be an educator at an alternative high school. Those charged with championing the world's youths are shown how to thoughtfully approach difficult interactions.

Aug. 2023 Release!

Length: 74 pages
Size: 6x9 inches
Paperback ISBN: 978-1954819917 ($12. 99)

Young Adult Books

Spotlight Title

Gripped Part 1: The Truth We Never Told
by Stacy A. Padula

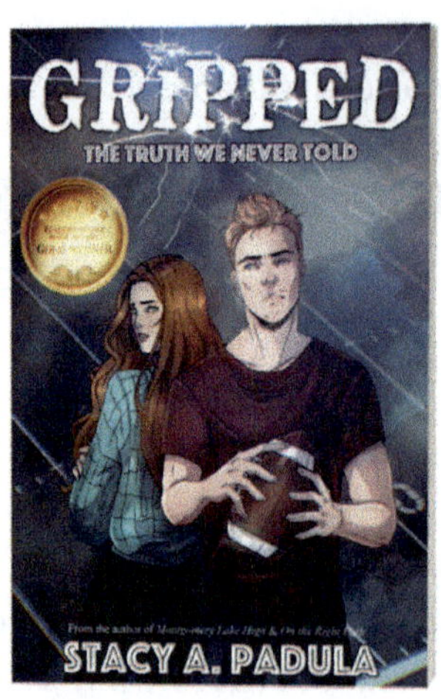

In high school, Taylor Dunkin broke more records than any other athlete to step foot in Montgomery, Massachusetts. As a sophomore in college, he was ranked by ESPN as one of the NFL's top 100 prospects. However, his aspirations came to a jarring halt when a season-ending injury sent him spiraling into a dark world of pain, depression, and addiction.

One year later, Taylor is a person of interest in a highly confidential investigation headed by the Boston Police Department. He has entangled himself in a crime ring notorious for pushing drugs on local college campuses. Montgomery's hometown hero has fallen hard, and he's taking a lot of people down with him.

Luke Davids has become the middleman between Taylor and teens in Montgomery who want to buy drugs. Freshmen Cathy Kagelli, Chris Dunkin, and Jason Davids are just a few of the students at Montgomery Lake High who have fallen victim to the benzos and opiates supplied by Taylor and Luke.

When Taylor's youngest brother Marc discovers that Taylor is behind the copious amount of pills circulating around his high school, he sets off to not only reverse the damage Taylor has caused, but also save his lifelong role model from becoming a casualty of America's deadly opioid epidemic.

Size: 6x9 inches
Length: 210 pages
Paperback ISBN: 978-1735016832 ($16.95)
Hardcover ISBN: 978-1733153638 ($24.95)

The Gold Winner for "Best Teen Book"—now being adapted for TV by Emmy® award-winning producer Mark Blutman!

Gripped Part 2: Blindsided
by Stacy A. Padula

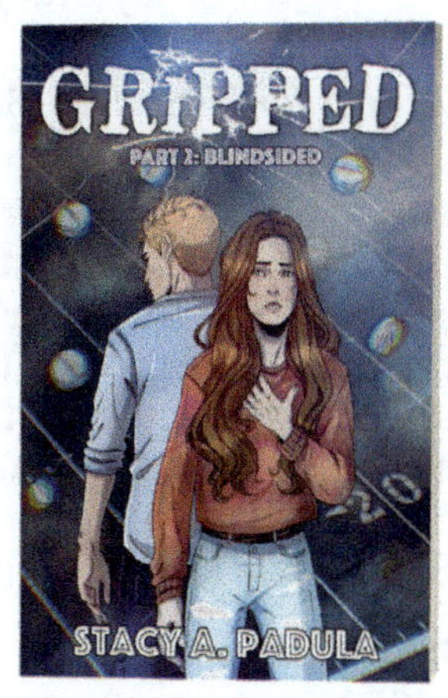

Fourteen-year-old Chris Dunkin is known for being the life of the party and everyone's favorite friend. Despite his amicable nature, he carries around deep-seated pain from his childhood that he frequently numbs with alcohol and drugs. After hosting a party, Chris awakes with no recollection of the previous night. When he learns the horrifying truth of what his night entailed, the trajectory of his life is changed forever.

Length: 186 pages
Size: 6x9 inches
Hardcover ISBN: 978-1735016801 ($24.95)
Paperback ISBN: 978-1733153607 ($16. 95)

Gripped Part 3: The Fallout
by Stacy A. Padula

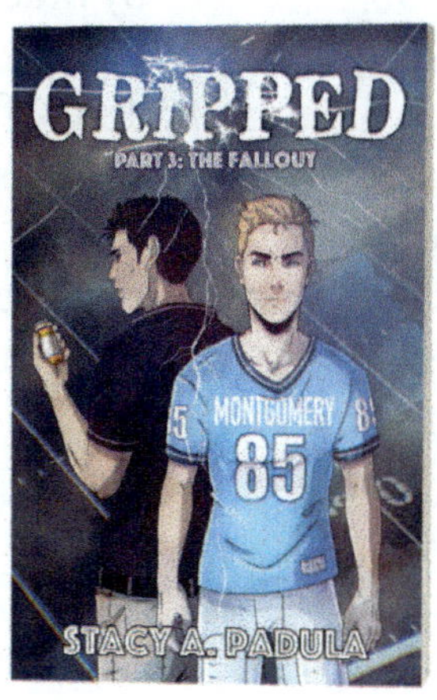

After a near-death experience, Chris Dunkin begins surrounding himself with positive influences and putting his efforts towards living a clean lifestyle. Meanwhile, Marc Dunkin has received word from a detective that his oldest brother Taylor is a person of interest in a highly confidential case headed by the Boston Police Department. They know Taylor's clean; they know he wants out of the game; and they want to help make that happen. However, their "help" may put Taylor and his entire family in grave danger.

Length: 160 pages
Size: 6x9 inches
Hardcover ISBN: 978-1735016818 ($24.95)
Paperback ISBN: 978-1733153621 ($16. 95)

Gripped Part 4: Smoke & Mirrors
by Stacy A. Padula

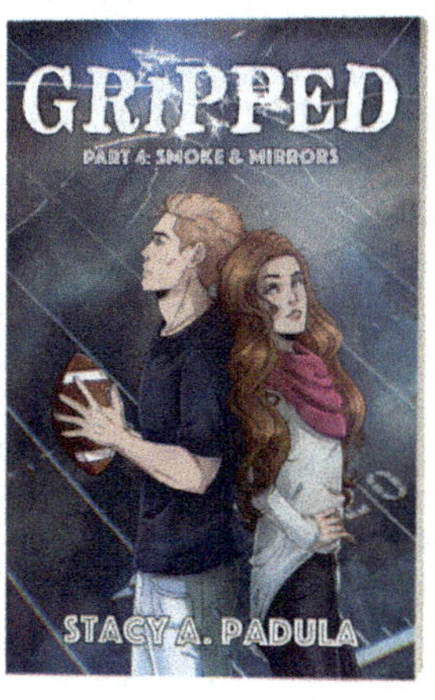

Taylor Dunkin is used to high stakes. As an NCAA star quarterback, he performed under pressure to lead his team to victory, but his football career came to an abrupt halt when an injury sent him spiraling down a dark hole of pain, depression, and addiction. Now he finds himself playing a game with even higher stakes because his life, his reputation, and the safety of everyone he loves are all on the line. In Taylor's weakest moment, he made a deal with the devil, and now there is a reckoning. But who will pay the price?

Length: 274 pages
Size: 6x9 inches
Hardcover ISBN: 978-1735016825 ($28.95)
Paperback ISBN: 978-1733153645 ($18. 95)

Gripped Part 5: Taylor's Story
by Stacy A. Padula

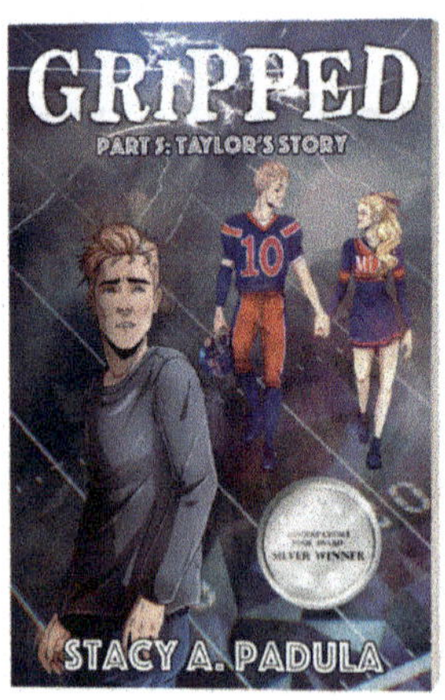

The Silver Winner for "Best Teen Book" in the 2022 Readers' Choice Book Awards!

Taylor Dunkin is missing. The last message Jordan Dunkin receives from Taylor leads him to Taylor's abandoned Jeep. Each of Taylor's family members holds a piece of the puzzle, and as the Dunkins begin putting the details together, they are awakened to the possibility they may never see Taylor again.

Length: 232 pages
Size: 6x9 inches
Hardcover ISBN: 978-1954819252 ($24.95)
Paperback ISBN: 978-1954819245 ($16. 95)

Montgomery Lake High #1: The Right Person
by Stacy A. Padula

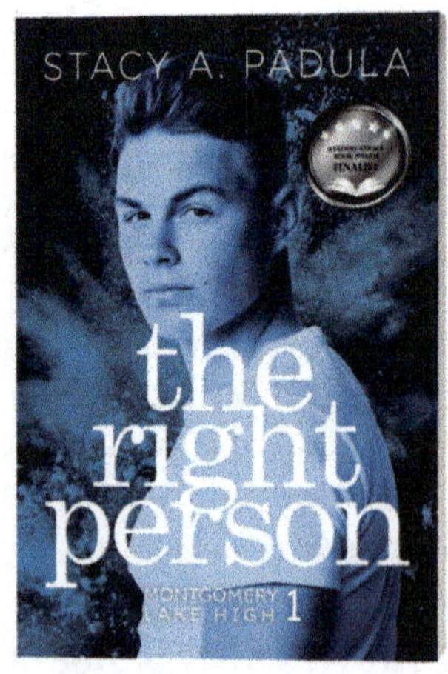

Growing up in the shadow of two NFL-destined cousins, Chris Dunkin has high hopes for his own future in football. However, a drug addiction threatens to destroy everything he has worked hard to attain. When Chris meets Courtney Angeletti—the mayor's straightedge Christian daughter—he believes she could be the source of inspiration he needs to overcome his destructive lifestyle.

Length: 164 pages
Size: 6x9 inches
Paperback ISBN: 978-1735016849 ($13.95)
Hardcover ISBN: 978-1733153652 ($24.95)

Montgomery Lake High #2: When Darkness Tries to Hide
by Stacy A. Padula

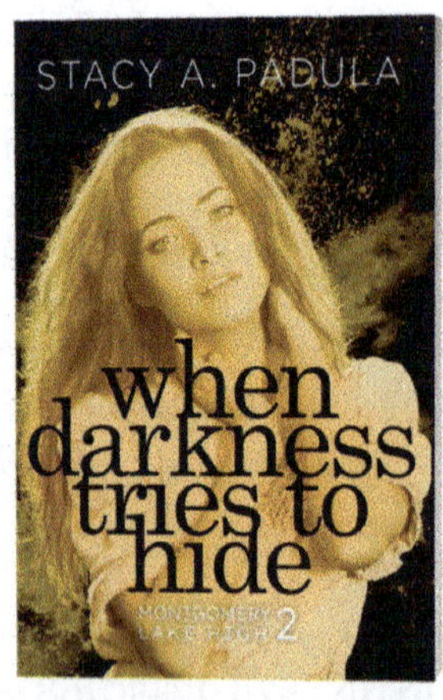

Students at Montgomery Lake High believe the ominous clouds and impending storm will only bring a temporary interruption to their regularly scheduled lives. However, when the tempest grows worse and a classmate's life hangs in the balance, students must pull together to seek help for their friend. As the lines between cliques dissolve, dark secrets are revealed and hearts are transformed.

Length: 164 pages
Size: 6x9 inches
Paperback ISBN: 978-1735016856 ($16.95)
Hardcover ISBN: 978-1733153669 ($24.95)

  www.brileybaxterbooks.com | wholesale distribution through Ingram

Montgomery Lake High #3: The Aftermath
by Stacy A. Padula

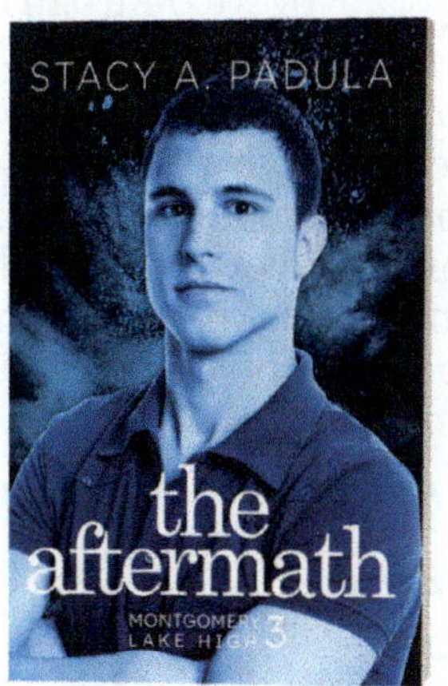

At age fifteen, Jason Davids appears to have nearly any worldly thing that promises enjoyment at his disposal. After failing to fill the void with achievements, relationships, and illicit substances, Jason finds himself intrigued by Jessie Robins: the daughter of a local pastor. How is it possible that she stands for everything his lifestyle opposes yet possesses the one thing he has been searching for all along?

Length: 190 pages
Size: 6x9 inches
Paperback ISBN: 978-1735016863 ($16.95)
Hardcover ISBN: 978-1735016863 ($24.95)

Montgomery Lake High #4: The Battle for Innocence
by Stacy A. Padula

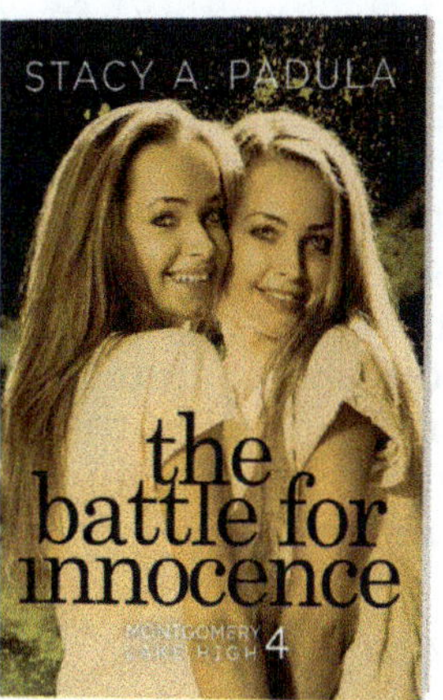

Jon Anderson and Chantal Kagelli are trying to live moral lives, but temptations are plaguing them in and out of school. Will they continue to be lights in their best friends' lives or will they get pulled into the darkness?

Length: 152 pages
Size: 6x9 inches
Paperback ISBN: 978-1735016870 ($14.95)
Hardcover ISBN: 978-1733153683 ($24.95)

Montgomery Lake High #5: The Forces Within
by Stacy A. Padula

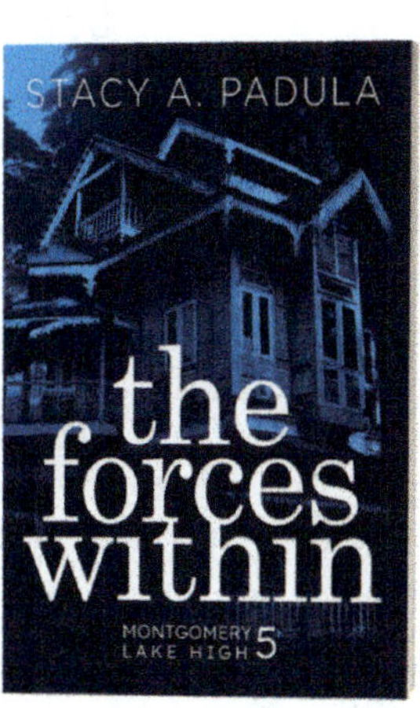

After being trapped inside his own body, unable to communicate with anyone but his own thoughts, Andy Rosetti finally wakes up from the coma that controlled his life for one month. Upon awakening, Andy finds himself and his friends in a mansion riddled with secret passages and supernatural forces. Andy must figure out if the darkness lies within the mansion's walls or within the people surrounding him.

Length: 158 pages
Size: 6x9 inches
Paperback ISBN: 978-1735016887 ($16.95)
Hardcover ISBN: 978-1733153690 ($24.95)

10% of publishing royalties are donated to animal rescues

Boy to Successful Man: A Roadmap for Teens & Young Adults
by Rico Austin & Dr. Suave Powers

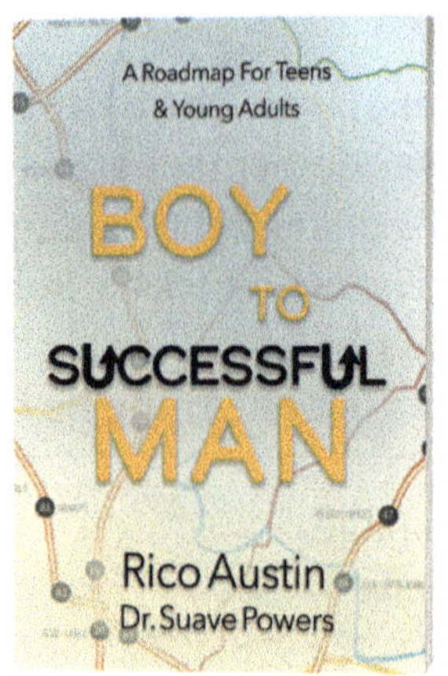

If you have ever sat at the knees of a family member or neighbor who regaled you with their wild stories and hard-earned lessons, you have probably learned a thing or two about how others' stories can help prepare you for life. Through Boy to Successful Man, you will gain invaluable information from two authors who have seen it all. This book is a tool to give young men great lives, no matter their circumstances.

Length: 104 pages
Size: 6x9 inches
Paperback ISBN: 978-1954819122 ($13.99)

Penikese Island Adventure
by Kathleen Hickey

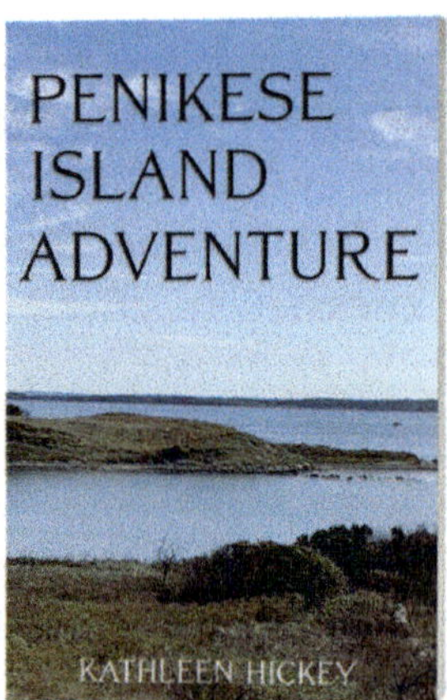

When Julia plans to spend the summer with her dad in New York City, the last thing she expects is to be drawn into a mysterious and exciting adventure on an abandoned island off the coast of Massachusetts. Her father's work leads him to serve as the head psychologist at a camp on Penikese Island—the home to twelve troubled boys and a limited staff. What Julia expects to be a boring summer ends up being the adventure of a lifetime, as she finds herself caught up in a forgotten mystery, hidden danger, and a forbidden romance.

Length: 142 pages
Size: 6x9 inches
Paperback ISBN: 978-1954819054 ($14.99)

Inherently Fallible
by Shawn Janes

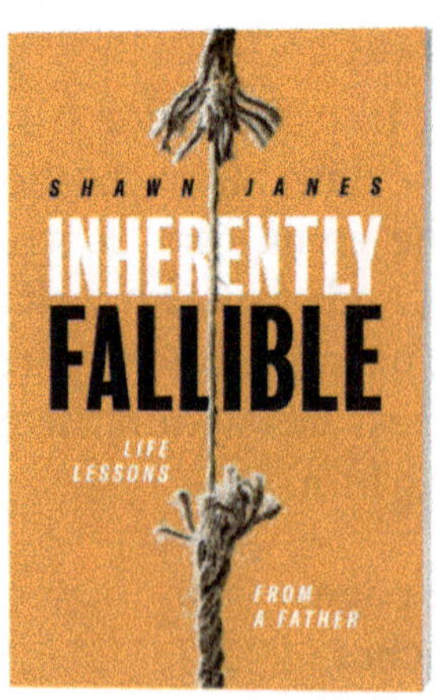

There is a maddening truth that only parents know about the unsolicited advice we offer our children. Although shared with hopes of preventing our children from reliving our mistakes, it seems to merge with everything else as it passes through one ear and out the other, lost in their internal hard drive and often followed by the infamous eye roll. That is, of course, until they get the same advice from someone else. That was the catalyst for this book: creating a tangible reference of life lessons for young adults—everything I wish I knew before age twenty-five.

Length: 68 pages
Size: 6x9 inches
Paperback ISBN: 978-1954819061 ($12.99)

Stars of the North
by Lucy Kovaliv

The Iditarod—to most people, it's an exciting and exotic dogsled race through the toughest terrain in Alaska, but for Bill O'Malley, it's a mission of redemption. Meanwhile, his daughter Puck, son Joseph, and their friend Mary face challenges of their own with Dad away. A mysterious house with a dark past beckons them into rule-breaking and scary encounters with new and old enemies. Stars of the North is a thrilling tale of life in the snowiest parts of the Yukon and Alaska, where survival means depending on your family, your friends, and most of all, your instincts.

Length: 202 pages
Size: 6x9 inches
Paperback ISBN: 978-1954819450 ($16.95)

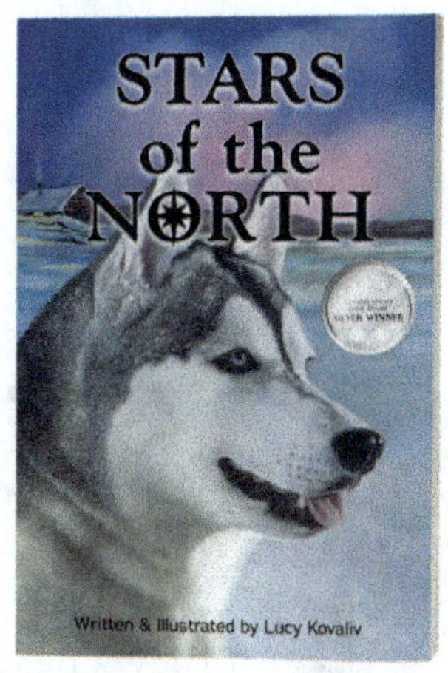

The Crash
by Isabelle Semas

Phybe has always known a life of peace. After World War III, she and her family are cared for by the United Lands Government Organization (ULGO). When Phybe's brother Merek comes home from officer training, Phybe perceives trouble on the horizon. Meanwhile, Taelor has spent most of his life trying to keep his younger brother and sister safe as they live among ULGO outcasts known as Variables. When Taelor's sister is taken by service workers, he and his brother must embark on a mission to rescue her.

Length: 236 pages
Size: 6x9 inches
Paperback ISBN: 978-1954819184 ($16.95)

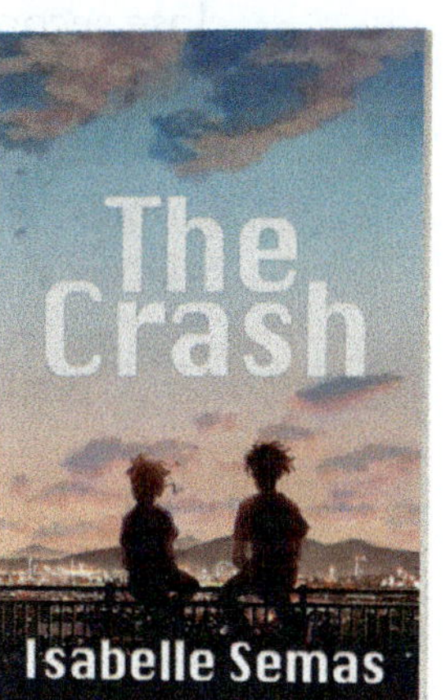

What Came After
by Tabor Millien

To outsiders, Hannah has it all. She's taking college classes, holding down a fun job, and dating one of the most sought-after boys in town. But Hannah has secrets—secrets about herself and her past, the people she's hurt, and the people who want to hurt her. When an unthinkable tragedy blurs the line between the natural and the supernatural, Hannah finds herself trapped between the world of the living and the dead.

Length: 188 pages
Size: 6x9 inches
Paperback ISBN: 978-1954819863 ($16.95)

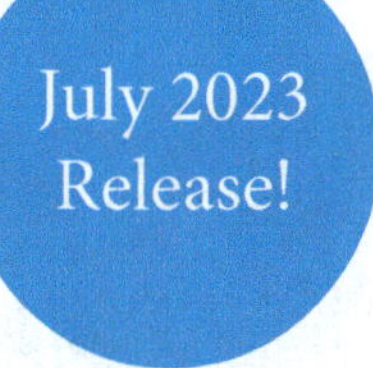

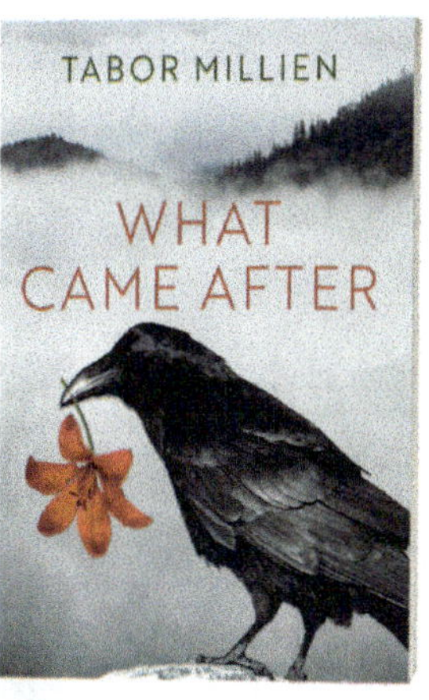

10% of publishing royalties are donated to animal rescues

About Briley & Baxter

Briley & Baxter are miniature dachshunds from Plymouth, Massachusetts. They live with their parents, Stacy and Tim, in the Pinehills.

Briley is eighteen years old, but he is still full of energy, pep, and joy! He loves nothing more than being on his mom's lap—but eating treats is a close second!

Baxter is nine years old. He loves to play catch, cuddle, & meet new people. He was rescued as a puppy from P.S. I Love You Animal Rescue in Arkansas.

Briley & Baxter go to the office every day with their mom and love meeting authors, staff, and clients. Their adventures can be followed on their Instagram @two_cuddly_dachshunds. Their TwoCuddlyDachshunds Etsy Shop donates 50% of its proceeds to animal rescues each month.

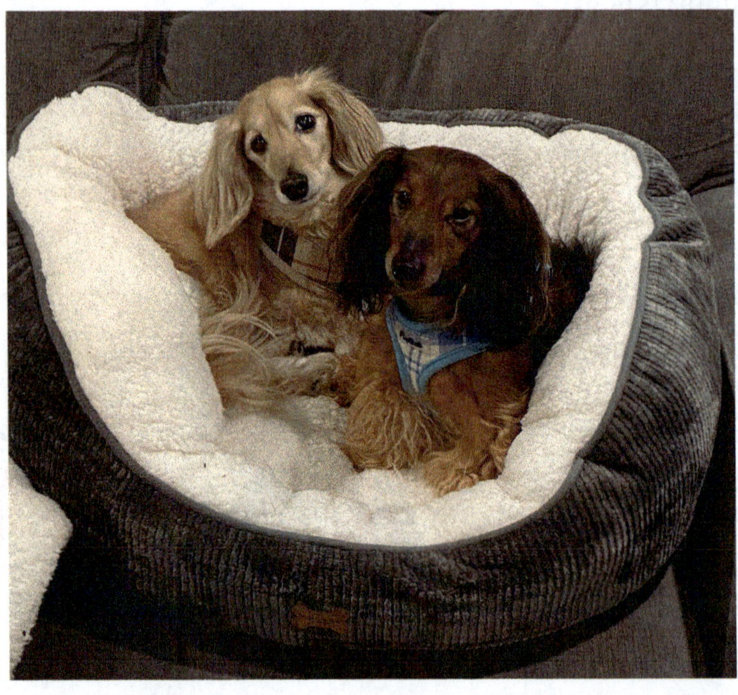

Printed by BoD™in Norderstedt, Germany